TOP YOUTUBE STARS™

BETHANY MOTA

Style Icon with More than 900 MILLION VIEWS

KATHY FURGANG

D1625597

rosen publishing's
rosen central®

New York

For my nieces, Liz, Jen, and Sidney

Published in 2020 by The Rosen Publishing Group, Inc.
29 East 21st Street, New York, NY 10010

Copyright © 2020 by The Rosen Publishing Group, Inc.

First Edition

All rights reserved. No part of this book may be reproduced in any form without permission in writing from the publisher, except by a reviewer.

Library of Congress Cataloging-in-Publication Data

Names: Furgang, Kathy, author.
Title: Bethany Mota: Style Icon with More than 900 Million Views / Kathy Furgang.
Description: First edition. | New York : Rosen Central, 2020. | Series: Top YouTube stars | Includes bibliographical references and index.
Identifiers: LCCN 2018051570| ISBN 9781725346192 (library bound) | ISBN 9781725346185 (pbk.)
Subjects: LCSH: Mota, Bethany, 1995– —Juvenile literature. | Internet personalities—United States—Biography—Juvenile literature. | YouTube (Electronic resource)—Biography—Juvenile literature.
Classification: LCC PN2287.M775 F76 2019 | DDC 791.092 [B]—dc23
LC record available at https://lccn.loc.gov/2018051570

Manufactured in the United States of America

On the cover: On October 7, 2014, YouTube style queen Bethany Mota arrives at the Los Angeles premiere of *The Best of Me* by Relativity Studios.

CONTENTS

INTRODUCTION

I f you were born after the year 2000, chances are you are much more familiar with YouTube than traditional television and radio. Maybe you already know that today's YouTube watchers have a chance of becoming tomorrow's YouTube stars. YouTube has an average of a billion video views on mobile devices every day, according to the website Brandwatch. Brandwatch also reports that six out of ten people prefer watching video platforms such as YouTube over television. YouTube has been able to deliver for these viewers by providing content in seventy-six languages and being available in more than eighty-eight countries. YouTube has even become a search engine for people looking for media content. People search for "how to" videos, music, comedy, news events, or pop culture "trending" events they may have missed.

One of the most innovative things about YouTube is that the viewers can become the creators. Anyone can start a YouTube channel. Four hundred hours of video are uploaded to the website per minute. A number of the people uploading videos are hoping to make money off the views. Advertising on the site has paid out billions of dollars to people running YouTube channels. That's because the people watching the videos will also be seeing the advertising on the page. YouTube stars with a large following have a lot of advertising power.

Since YouTube first launched in 2005, advertisers have been eyeing the platform. Advertising was first introduced in 2007, and over the past decade YouTube has dominated the market and allowed for a brand-new kind of millionaire—a YouTube sensation.

Users with YouTube channels have made an art out of getting subscribers and corporate sponsors. They collect money from advertising that is viewed on their videos, and corporate sponsors pay them to display or discuss their products. A person who creates content for YouTube is called a YouTuber, or a YouTube personality. The most successful of these become celebrities due to a high number of sub-scribers. Bethany Mota is one of these YouTube sensations, with more than ten million subscrib-ers. Mota has created a popular online person-ality by being herself as she gives advice about fashion and self-esteem, or "positivity." Since starting her YouTube channel when she was thirteen, she has learned to make YouTube into a career and a profitable business. She has paired with fashion lines and put popular makeup and fashion brands in the spotlight for her viewers. Mota has also brought YouTube stars into the mainstream. In 2014, she

After starting a YouTube channel at age thirteen, Bethany Mota went on to become a YouTube sensation and an inspiration to millions of her young followers.

became the first YouTuber to be cast on *Dancing with the Stars*. Today she continues posting about travel, cooking, and anything else that interests her.

Other YouTube sensations have become rich and famous because of their videos of themselves playing video games, talking about sports, or just recording and talking about their own lives. Viewers and subscribers find it easy to relate to the content because they feel it is authentic. In the case of Bethany Mota's viewers, they feel her posts are like watching a message from a friend because they are natural and she talks about things they are interested in. Viewers want to know about her life, which is just what the following pages explore.

CHAPTER ONE

Young Bethany

B ethany Mota was born on November 7, 1995, in California. Her parents, Tony and Tammy, come from a Mexican and Portuguese background. Mota has an older sister named Brittany. Born into an age of internet technologies, Mota has grown up familiar with all things digital. YouTube was started when Mota was just nine years old.

Much of the details about Bethany Mota's childhood are explained on her YouTube video "Draw My Life." The Draw My Life videos are a popular medium for YouTube stars and many other celebrities to tell their own life story through playful stick-figure drawings on a whiteboard, with the celebrity narrating details of important childhood events. In 2013, Mota's YouTube fans asked her to post her own "Draw My Life" video.

In the video, Mota described having a happy childhood growing up in Los Banos, California, with her parents and her sister Brittany, who is five years older than her. She recalled fun times traveling on family vacations to Disneyland, and spending time with her extended family, including her many cousins. She recalled that her family moved when she was

Los Banos is located in central California, in the San Joaquin Valley. Mota grew up there with her parents and older sister.

five years old to "a small house in the middle of nowhere" with lots of animals around. Mota's mother schooled the two girls at home, and she recalls her sister Brittany being a much better student than she was. Mota required her mother's help with school work much more often than her sister had. One of Mota's favorite things to do as a homeschooled student was to watch *Arthur* at lunchtime.

Mota described herself as very shy. Although she had a best friend named Alyssa who she felt comfortable with, she did not speak to many other people and claimed that some people

HOMESCHOOLING

Homeschooling is the practice of being schooled away from a traditional classroom environment, at home, led by parents. The practice is growing throughout North America, as well as in parts of Europe and Asia. Homeschooling allows parents to decide with their children what kind of education is best for them and customize the education to fit the student's needs. In the United States, many states require homeschooled students to cover many of the same topics as classroom students, and some require them to take state tests. However, there is more freedom for the child to pursue special interests or take part in education that may be part of the child's special interest or the family's belief systems. Homeschooled students can also work at their own pace and socialize with other homeschooled students in extracurricular activities. The decision to homeschool is often based on a family's opinions about their public school and its resources, their community environment, or the child's social or academic development.

thought she was mute because she never spoke. She even recalls being very shy in front of some of her own extended family members.

OFF TO PUBLIC SCHOOL

When Mota was in third grade, her sister was in eighth grade. That year, her sister expressed a desire to go to public school.

Her mother tried to convince Mota to go too, and she reluctantly agreed. The sisters went to different schools, however, which was difficult for Mota. While Brittany went to a middle school, Bethany went to an elementary school. Starting at the school in the middle of the school year made it even more difficult for the already shy and struggling student.

While third grade was difficult, Mota claims that she had an easier time in fourth grade because she met two girls who

Bethany Mota began her YouTube channel after enduring online bullying. She hoped her experience would help others as well as build up her own confidence and self-esteem.

became her best friends. By the time she started middle school in sixth grade, she was excited to start at a new school. However, she started to drift apart from her two best friends because they were assigned to many of the same classes together, but Mota was not in the classes with them. Mota decided to join the cheerleading squad to try to meet some new people. She enjoyed the experience and met two new friends. However, those girls did not attend the same school as she did, so she did not get to see them as much as she wanted. Her experiences in middle school were not going as well as she had hoped.

By Christmas vacation, Mota explained in her "Draw My Life" video, her grandfather passed away and she was feeling even more sad and lonely. She requested that she go back to being homeschooled, and her mother agreed.

A DIFFICULT TIME

During this same difficult time, when she was twelve, Mota experienced online bullying by people she knew from school. In an interview with the Build Series YouTube Channel in 2017, Mota explained that she had never felt a lack of confidence about her appearance or body until her peers started criticizing her. She said the experience with cyberbullying and body shaming led her into a difficult time because she was already a shy person.

In a 2015 interview on *The Ellen DeGeneres Show*, she explained that people she knew from school started a fake Myspace page of her identity to make fun of her physical appearance. "It was people that I actually knew," she said about the fake page. "It was my face and my name, but it was almost like I was making fun of myself. All the captions were about my physical appearance and just me making fun of who I was."

MYSPACE

Today's young social media users are most familiar with communicating on Instagram, SnapChat, Facebook, and other platforms. In 2007, however, MySpace was the most popular social media website. Today MySpace is known more as a social media platform for music lovers, but it was the most popular general social media site before Facebook became popular in 2008. Bethany Mota's experience with the site in 2007 shows that cyberbullying and body shaming has been a problem online for more than a decade, and its effects can even outlast the popularity of the social media platform itself.

BUILDING CONFIDENCE

As part of her homeschooling, Mota took part in activities that she hoped would help her shyness and anxiety. She started taking acting classes and dance classes. She explained in her "Draw My Life" video that she really enjoyed taking part in the dance competitions, making new friends, and dressing up in costumes for competitions. She also had fun acting and singing in a production of the musical *Annie.*

Her anxiety and depression returned, however. Online bullies had turned two of her good friends against her. She began to have trouble eating. She also had anxiety attacks that caused her to quit dancing and acting because she had trouble leaving the house.

Mota's YouTube channel included "haul" videos, in which she unpacked, displayed, and discussed purchases, such as new clothing and makeup.

One way she helped cope with her problem was to watch You-Tube videos. She found a beauty community that she enjoyed and spent a lot of time watching the videos. Eventually, she decided that it might help her deal with her insecurity and anxiety issues if she posted some of her own videos on YouTube. So in 2009, she started a YouTube channel called Macbarbie07. She then filmed and posted her first video on June 12. In the seven-minute video, called "First Video :) Mac and Sephora Haul," she describes her recent makeup purchases. Mota didn't know it at the time, but it was the first step to becoming a YouTube sensation and a role model to countless teens and pre-teens. Today Mota has more than ten million subscribers and more than four hundred videos that have received a total of close to a billion views.

CHAPTER TWO

Starting Out on YouTube

C ompared to the Bethany Mota that young people follow on YouTube today, her first post on her channel Macbarbie07 shows just how far the star has come. While her bubbly personality can be seen in her seven-minute "haul" video, the thirteen-year-old's insecurity shows also. Throughout the video she posts notes on the screen with apologies about the sound and the video quality. At one point in the video she even apologizes for the chair she is sitting on making squeaking noises. In the caption under the video, it says, "This is my first video :)sorry if I was kinda quite.. i was tired lol! If you have any requests please let me know and I will try to get to them! :)) xoxo god bless."

Mota has come a long way since that first video. Knowing the reason she started the YouTube channel in the first place—as a response to online bullying she had experience and to give herself courage—she speaks with considerable confidence. In her "Draw My Life" video, she says that she simply set her camera up on a stack of books in her bedroom for that first shoot because she did not have a tripod to mount her camera on.

She speaks for seven minutes, displaying for the camera her new Mac makeup and Sephora purchases, explaining each item

Mota started out making videos in which she applied makeup. By 2015, others sometimes applied her makeup, as shown here before the Go Red for Women fashion show in New York City.

and why she chose it. Her explanations include when she plans to use the makeup, and why its color is a good choice for her. Her detailed descriptions include why she likes a product's new applicator shape more than the old one, and why she chooses one brand to replace another one she doesn't like.

In 2009, "haul" videos were just beginning to become popular. They were a reason many people started to subscribe and watch YouTube videos in the first place. The honest and practical advice and product reviews attracted not only viewers, but advertisers and corporate sponsors who want to get their products in the hands of customers.

In an interview with Lindsey Seavert in *USA Today*, Mota recalled the empowering feeling of posting that first video and gaining back her confidence. "I just became hooked," she said. She recalled thinking to herself, "I can create whatever I want, have these ideas and put it out there. I have this voice and opinion again."

GETTING NOTICED ON YOUTUBE

In an interview on *The Ellen DeGeneres Show* in 2015, Mota recalled what it was like to try to get an audience on YouTube. She said that with so many other people uploading videos to the site it's very hard to get noticed. She recalled returning to her own video over and over to see if more people were viewing it. When she noticed the count slowly increasing she got excited. It did not take long for her to realize that the count was including her own views and that she was one of the only people—besides her mother—who was viewing the video. With some patience and persistence, however, that changed and she grew a fan base and subscribership.

Mota continued vlogging, or video blogging. She uploaded more videos of her fashion hauls and makeup and haircare tutorials. Her video views and subscribership slowly increased, and she continued to consistently try to make videos that would attract newer subscribers. She stuck to the format of other

Singer Selena Gomez, shown here, is admired for her beautiful makeup, among other things. One of Mota's earliest tutorials on YouTube described how to apply eye makeup like that worn by Gomez in a music video.

beauty and fashion YouTube videos at the time, which were becoming very popular.

The first of Mota's videos to have a thousand views was a makeup tutorial that showed viewers how to apply eye makeup like Selena Gomez had worn in a recent video. Because the video was already a trending topic online, it attracted more viewers who searched the topic. Mota realized that in order to be seen by more people, she needed to pair her themes and topics with topics people were already looking for. For this reason, she posted videos with holiday themes, back-to-school themes, and beauty tips for trending categories in fashion. According to an article from thinkwithgoogle.com, this strategy helped Mota reach a milestone of one million views per month in 2010 with her Halloween-themed posts. By the next year, she was up to about five million views per month.

Mota continues to be one of the most popular YouTube personalities at back-to-school time and collects the biggest number of new subscribers at that time of the year. Young people looking for new back-to-school clothes and fashion advice find her videos easily. According to research about how people use YouTube, thinkwithgoogle.com data shows that Mota's back-to-school videos provide her with one-and-a-half times as many "likes" and new subscribers than videos with other topics.

In 2010, Mota decided to focus her YouTube strategy even more. She changed the name of her channel from Macbarbie07 to Bethany Mota, which helped to make her name more recognizable. She then started another YouTube channel called Bethany's Life that would focus more on her personal life than beauty and fashion vlogging. She posted videos there related to travel, cooking, and anything else that interested her. That channel has more than two million subscribers, while her original Bethany Mota channel currently has more than ten million subscribers.

A SELF-TAUGHT SENSATION

After Mota's first video in which she apologized for the poor sound and quality, she slowly taught herself to improve the videos she posts. In an interview by Helin Jung with *Cosmopolitan*, she was asked how she transitioned in to more polished videos. She replied, "I haven't taken one editing class. I've learned everything on my own. If I didn't know how to do something, I'd Google it. That's what I think is also inspiring for people to watch, is that they can do this too. I built it on my own and this is something that everyone is capable of doing." Her videos include introductions, music, and simple special effects. She went on to say that her fans also like to see the "more candid side" of her life. When she posted a blooper clip once, she learned that fans enjoyed that. She realized, "they really want to see who you are as a person, what you like, what you dislike, your imperfections, your mess-ups. That's what makes you real."

CONNECTING WITH VIEWERS

As her popularity on YouTube increased, Mota wanted to connect with her fans, who she refers to as "friends" and "Mota-vators." In addition to her fashion and beauty videos, Mota uploads videos that try to promote confidence in her viewers. In 2010, she posted the video "You're Not Alone," because she said many of her viewers posted comments to tell her that they were victims of bullying. She wanted to address them and give them advice to let them know that many people experience the same problem

Part of Mota's appeal to young people is that she provides inspiring messages and encourages her followers to believe in themselves. She speaks at festivals and conferences about confidence.

and that they should not care what other people think about them. She hinted that she had been cyber-bullied herself, but did not give specifics about her situation. She wrote underneath the title of the video, "I really wanted to do this because it is requested daily."

Then in 2011, she posted the video "Confidence," which starts with a quote from Dr. Seuss on the screen, which says, "Be who you are and say what you feel because those who mind don't matter and those who matter don't mind." She then talks about the importance of having confidence in ourselves. She recommends not looking to other people for reassurance about confidence. She says that it must come from within ourselves instead of from others. She wrote underneath the title of the video, "even if this inspires just one person that would make me ecstatic." At the end of the video, she asks viewers to post a comment naming something they like about themselves and something they don't like about themselves. Nearly seven thousand comments were left by people responding to her request and replying to the video's content.

The connection to her fans, or "friends," is important to her, and she has said in interviews, including a recorded interview with the *Today* show in 2014, that she takes her fans' comments seriously and often uses their comments to give her ideas about what to include in her videos.

CHAPTER THREE

Star Status

Once Bethany Mota became a YouTube sensation, she expanded her reach beyond YouTube. In December 2013, Mota partnered with fashion corporations JC Penney and Forever 21 to launch a line of clothing, perfume, and accessories. She also partnered with the teen clothing store Aéropostale to create accessories that are branded with her name. After the first line was introduced by Aéropostale, she continued to create apparel for them, working with their designers to present apparel that reflected her style. According to a 2016 article by Mallory Schlossberg in Business Insider, Mota created lines for the company for three years and was even considered to be one of the business ventures that the company hoped would help boost sales. Similar to the way she attracted viewers to her YouTube channel, Mota attracted fashion shoppers with several popular holiday-themed lines of clothing and accessories.

Mota's business partnerships were made possible by her success on YouTube. The teen continued to gain exposure outside of YouTube. In 2014, she was a guest judge on *Project Runway* and became the first YouTube star to be chosen to compete on the television show *Dancing with the Stars.* That

Mota greets fans when she appears at public events, such as this 2013 mall event in Chicago, Illinois.

year, Mota also received the Teen Choice Award for Most Popular Female Web Star, as well as the Streamy Award for Best Fashion Show. Perhaps her most high-profile accomplishment of that year was being named among *Time* magazine's 25 most influential teens of the year. She was on the list along with first daughters Sasha and Malia Obama, actors Rico Rodriguez, Jaden Smith, and Chloë Grace Moretz, reality stars Kylie and Kendal Jenner, singer Lorde, and Nobel Peace Prize winner Malala Yousafzai.

Mota even appeared on the cover of *Seventeen* magazine. In the September 10, 2014, article, she explained how having a YouTube channel since she was thirteen helped her business-sense as she grew up. She replied, "I think it's taught me to be a lot more self-motivated and has taught me how to encourage myself and not rely on a teacher or a boss telling me what to do. I'm my own boss." She also included her signature message about being yourself. "My biggest thing to overcome," she continued, "has been not being afraid to be different. It's safer to do what everyone else is doing, but it pays off way more to be yourself." And even though she was branching off into new business ventures beyond YouTube, she was sure to shout out appreciation to her loyal fans. "I wouldn't say that my viewers on YouTube are any less my friends than my real-life friends. If anything," she

REALITIES OF THE BUSINESS WORLD

Becoming a famous success in the media and business world can have its downsides as well. In 2017, Mota was hired by a marketing company to promote a skincare product across social media sites. The company flew Mota and her father to Hawaii for an exciting backdrop for Mota's film shoots. The company, however, was not pleased with the results and claimed that Mota did not fulfill her obligations. As a result, they sued her and her father, who was also her manager. The case is still pending, but it shows the risk that some YouTubers may face when reviewing or working with products from large companies or when expected to deliver for corporate sponsors.

said, "they understand me better. Sometimes I open up more to my viewers because I can help them if they're going through the same situation."

MUSICAL MOTA-VATION

In addition to appearing on *Dancing with the Stars* to showcase her dancing abilities, Mota made a 2014 pop single, "Need You Right Now." She explained to Arial Nagi of *Seventeen* magazine that she wrote the song to express her personal experiences, but that it's not about any particular person. She said that it is about losing someone and struggling because of that loss because you still feel dependent on the person. She told the magazine she had been wanting to get into music for several years, and was pleased at the positive response.

Bethany Mota attended a YouTube event at Madison Square Garden in New York City. The event celebrated YouTube brands such as Mota's.

In August 2015, Mota posted a song called "Be Who You Wanna Be." She co-wrote the song and sang the acoustic ballad about the pressures of society to be or act a certain way.

Mota continues to explore her love for music, and was an award presenter at the 2016 iHeartRADIO MuchMusic Video Awards in Toronto, Canada.

Bethany Mota appears at public events to promote humanitarian efforts. In 2016, she attended a unite4:humanity event in Beverly Hills, California.

A CHAT WITH THE PRESIDENT

After the 2015 State of the Union address, President Barack Obama sat down with three YouTube stars to answer questions for their fans. Bethany Mota was one of the three people chosen to interview the president, along with GloZell, a rapper and comedian, and Hank Green, one half of the YouTube channel hosts of Vlogbrothers. During the January 22 show called "YouTube Asks Obama," the president praises the influence that the YouTube stars have with their online audience, and their chance to spread positive messages, explaining that they are "creating content with no barriers to entry."

In the video, Mota has a list of questions that her fans want to know about, including topics such as education, the economy, and unemployment. She asks the president first about how he hopes to make college education more affordable, which is a topic that's important to many of her young viewers. The president explains his policies while emphasizing that education is a key to the future for young people, and calls it "the best investment you can make."

Mota then reveals that even though she talks about her experiences with bullying and tries to motivate her online audience to feel confident in themselves, she can't always help them as much as she wants to. She asks the president how bullying in schools and online can be prevented in the first place. He replies that in this particular case, her experiences and work in the area of bullying prevention is even more influential than his as a president. He tells her that her position, influence, and experiences make her opinions respectable to people her age who are bullying or considering bullying their peers. He describes an antibullying conference made up of powerful organizations trying to stop the problem. But he says that the most influential and relatable people at the conference were the ones who had been through it themselves and were spreading the word about why it's unacceptable.

She then asks about raising awareness about international issues that young Americans may not be familiar with as much as they should be. This includes the influence of radical groups that spread hatred and international governments that control their citizens in ways that Americans are not aware of or alert to. Obama and Mota both encourage young people to become more alert of issues that impact people around the world. Obama describes involvement in politics in very simple terms, while also helping the audience see the impact of government in our lives. He explains that people becoming involved in politics must think

In 2015, Bethany Mota had the unique opportunity to interview President Barack Obama at the White House, along with other YouTube content creators.

of themselves as a group of friends trying to make a decision about what movie to go see. Because not everyone would want to see the same movie, you have to prepare an argument and reason to support the reason for going to the movie you want to see, and maybe compromise with friends. He says it's important to express your voice, your values, and what you care about so that you can live the life that you prefer to live. The compromises in politics are more complicated than ones done with friends and family, but the basics are the same so that people can live together in peace.

At the end of the interview Mota asks a series of fun, lightning round questions. Obama's answers reveal that his favorite thing to watch in his downtime is basketball or football, and that growing up he wanted to be an architect once he realized he would not make it as a professional basketball player. When asked what superpower he wishes he could have, he replies flying or speaking every language so he could speak to anyone he met in the world. The interview ends with Mota taking a group selfie with the president and the two other interviewers.

Mota vlogged about her trip to Washington on her Bethany's Life channel as she prepared for the interview and provided a separate link so her audience could watch the entire interview.

AN EYE FOR POSITIVITY

As Mota became successful with her various apparel brands and public appearances, she never forgot the reason that she posted her first video on YouTube. She continued to work to promote the idea of positivity in her business decisions, appearances, and products.

In October 2015, Mota paired with the PACER Center National Bullying Prevention Campaign and made a public appearance at Minneapolis, Minnesota's Mall of America. The appearance was to promote and support Unity Day. She made a short video,

ALL IN THE FAMILY

Bethany Mota has kept in close contact with her family throughout her time as a YouTube sensation and a business person. Her sister, Brittany, has her own YouTube channel and posts videos of her daughter Marin, who was born in 2012. Marin is frequently featured on her aunt Bethany's Instagram page and YouTube channel. When Mota interviewed President Barack Obama in 2015, she assembled a set to conduct the interview in front of. As part of the set, she put up a framed picture of herself with her niece so it could be seen behind the president during the filming.

which was posted as part of a *USA Today* article by Lindsey Seavert. The video explained her support for PACER, and revealed that she felt strongly about the antibullying message due to her own experiences with bullying. She encouraged people to get involved in antibullying events in their own communities.

Among her many achievements, Mota was asked in an interview what her greatest accomplishment has been so far. According to the *USA Today* article by Seavert, Mota says that it is her online community, whom she thinks of as a family. She expressed pride that her fans call themselves "Mota-vators." She said, "I am really happy they call themselves that because that is exactly what I want my channel and my audience to represent is just positivity and acceptance. I want to be able to create things so I can inspire people by doing what I love, it's the dream situation for me." She explained that "preaching self-love is so important. Instead of people putting you down, I think one of the best ways to fight that is to be sure of who you are, and to be confident in yourself, take care of your soul and take care of you."

This positive thinking is one of the biggest messages of her 2017 book, *Make Up Your Mind: My Guide to Finding Your Own Style, Life, and Motivation.* The book includes inspiration from her own life story, advice on love, living, creating your own style, and even recipes and DIY projects.

CHAPTER FOUR

Advice for Vlogging Mota-vators

With a billion hours of YouTube being watched every day, it's safe to say that the online platform is a good way to reach viewers. If you want to become a YouTuber there are two things to remember: there's nothing stopping you, *and* not every YouTuber has the same level of success. It's true that some YouTubers make millions of dollars per year uploading content to the channel. Those people, however, are extremely rare when you consider that there are about fifty million YouTube channels, according to the website Sidekick. Whether you are interested in starting a channel just for fun or in hopes of making money, there are some simple tips you can follow—some which even helped Bethany Mota succeed.

FOCUS YOUR IDEAS

While it's fun to just post to YouTube whatever videos you make with your friends, it helps to have a goal in mind if you want your channel to become popular. For example, Bethany Mota created content that fell under the category of "fashion and beauty."

Anyone can start a YouTube channel and upload content to the site. Follow the guidelines on the site for new users before starting a channel.

When she wanted to branch out and post lifestyle videos about travel, cooking, and DIY projects, she started another channel to keep the content separate. That approach can help attract more subscribers because it lets viewers know what to expect when they view new content. In other words, they know the new post will likely be something they're interested in.

Not all YouTubers need to follow a formula that already exists. You may just want your channel to have posts of school sporting events, performances, or assemblies. Or perhaps you want your channel to show how you assemble a model or make a painting, and have no intention of trying to attract other viewers besides friends and family. That's alright, too. The most useful channels are not always the ones with the most views or

STAY SAFE ONLINE

Being safe online is one of the most important tips for young YouTubers. It's a good idea to have a parent monitor your posts to make sure you are not accidentally revealing any personal information in your videos or comments. Don't give out personal information to anyone online. YouTube is a public website, so even posting personal information to a friend in a comment can be viewed by strangers. If you film your videos in your home, remember not to reveal your address or talk about local events that can give away your location or personal plans with friends.

subscribers, but the ones that set out to do what they intended to do.

If you are interested in attracting many subscribers and getting lots of views, however, try some strategies that helped Bethany Mota get started. She made her posts match the topics of other "trending," or popular, topics on YouTube. The first time she reached a thousand views was for a tutorial about how to apply eye makeup like Selena Gomez did in a recently released music video. Because the video was trending, she was able to make her own video trend as well. That upped her views. She repeated that with holiday and back-to-school posts. YouTube's "trending" section can help you find out what is popular right now. Even though trending topics change constantly, the viewers who see a video they like may choose to subscribe to your channel so they can see if they also like what you do in the future.

Not a lot of complicated equipment is required to start out filming and posting content to YouTube. Quality images can be created with a simple phone camera and tripod.

THE LOOK AND FEEL OF THE CHANNEL

Set up a YouTube channel only with the approval of a parent, and get any necessary technical help to upload videos. You don't need fancy equipment. Remember that Bethany Mota's first video was filmed on a camera that she propped on a stack of books on a desk in her bedroom. If you are able to either borrow or purchase your own equipment, a small tripod might be the most useful tool for setting up steady shots of yourself if you plan on talking directly into the camera.

Editing videos will require a decent computer that is not too old. It should be able to run video editing software. Try some free tools to get started, such as Windows Movie Maker or iMovie. While many professional YouTubers use the program Final Cut, it is not necessary for simple videos or for YouTubers just starting out. The program is harder to use and meant for professional editing.

In terms of investing money, a good microphone, camera, and lighting system are important. Look at YouTube videos that show how other YouTubers do it. Their tutorials can show you everything you need to know. Becoming comfortable with the technical side of creating content can allow you to focus more on the creative end.

Mota attended the 2nd Annual BeautyCon in New York City in 2015 to promote her fashion line at Aéropostale. She greeted fans at the event and posed for photos with them.

DEALING WITH NEGATIVE COMMENTERS

Whether your channel has one subscriber or one million, the chance of having negative or hateful comments about your videos exists. You can either choose to ignore the comments, or you can manage your account in ways that can control them. You can choose to disable, or not accept, the comments at all. This can be controlled in your account's default settings. Or, you can choose to moderate the comments. That means you can view the comments first and approve whether they can show on your page. If comments get through that you do not want to see, you can choose to delete them.

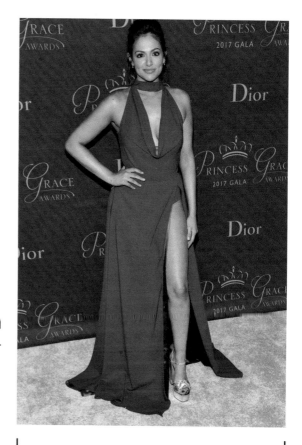

Mota attended the Princess Grace Awards Gala in 2017 in Beverly Hills, California.

Remember that it is important to think about not only the effect of negative posts about you and your videos, but it's also important to think about the negative effect that hurtful comments directed toward your other subscribers can be. Try to keep your comments section as constructive as possible. You may also choose to report negative behavior to YouTube. In addition, let an adult know about any threatening posts to your page.

THE ROAD TO CASHING IN

If you want to make money with your YouTube channel, you must reach the goals set up by YouTube to be considered in the YouTube Partner Program. The goals include having a channel with at least four thousand watched hours in the past twelve months, in addition to having at least a thousand subscribers. YouTube keeps track of the data related to every channel, and the owner of the channel can check his or her data to see how well his or her channel is doing over time. After a channel meets the requirements for the YouTube Partner Program, YouTube will consider your channel for monetization, or the ability to earn money from the channel. If your channel is accepted, you may set up an account with AdSense, which is needed for placing ads and transferring the money raised by those ads.

It can take a long time to become successful on YouTube, but the best advice is to be persistent. Think about the reason you want to be a YouTuber. If you are hoping to build your confidence like Bethany Mota did, and reach an audience who is similar to you, then YouTube can be a great venue. Take the advice that Mota gives her Mota-vators—whether you become a "sensation" or not, remember to feel confident about your efforts!

TIMELINE

1995 Bethany Mota is born on November 7 in California.

2006 Mota starts public school for the first time in third grade after being homeschooled.

2009 Mota starts homeschooling for the second time, in sixth grade.

2009 Mota starts her YouTube channel Macbarbie07 and posts her first haul video.

2010 For the first time, a Macbarbie07 post has a million views.

2010 Mota changes her YouTube channel name to Bethany Mota for fashion and beauty posts and begins the channel Bethany's Life as a lifestyle channel.

2013 Mota partners with JC Penney, Forever 21, and Aéropostale.

2014 Mota receives the Teen Choice Award for Most Popular Female Web Star and the Streamy Award for Best Fashion Show.

2014 Mota is featured on the cover of *Seventeen* magazine.

2014 Mota is the first YouTube star contestant on *Dancing with the Stars.*

2014 Mota releases her first music single, "Need You Right Now."

2015 Mota posts her second single, "Be Who You Wanna Be."

2015 Mota interviews President Barack Obama in the White House on January 22, along with YouTubers Hank Green and Glozell.

2016 Mota releases her final line of apparel with Aéropostale.

2017 Mota releases her first book, *Make Up Your Mind: My Guide to Finding Your Own Style, Life, and Motivation!*

GLOSSARY

blooper Video clips of errors.

body shaming Bullying or mistreatment regarding a person's body.

candid Not posed.

corporate sponsorship A form of advertising that promotes a product through an event or person who uses the product.

cyberbullying Bullying or mistreatment in an online venue.

default A computer or software setting that is preselected.

disable To make inactive or unusable.

DIY Do it yourself; the activity of making something yourself instead of buying it.

Final Cut A professional film editing program by Adobe.

haul video A type of video in which someone describes purchases.

iMovie A free video editing program by Apple.

moderate To monitor.

monetization The ability to turn a service into an exchange of money.

subscriber A person who signs up for a service.

trending A popular subject on social media.

tutorial A form of instruction in which a person models how to do something.

upload To transfer from a computer to the internet.

vlog Video log; online video posts.

Windows Movie Maker A free video editing program by Microsoft.

YouTuber A person who frequently posts to the video website YouTube.

FOR MORE INFORMATION

Canadian Centre for Child Protection

615 Academy Road
Winnipeg, MB R3N 0E7
Canada
(204) 945-5735
Website: https://www
.protectchildren.ca/en
Facebook: @Canadian
CentreForChildProtection
Twitter and Instagram:
@CdnChildProtect
The centre is a charity organization dedicated to protecting children against exploitation and victimization, including the effects of cyberbullying.

Canada Safety Council

1020 Thomas Spratt Place
Ottawa, ON K1G5L5
Canada
(613) 739-1535
Website: https://www
.canadasafetycouncil.org
Facebook: @canada.safety
Twitter: @CanadaSafetyCSC
The council provides support and tips for staying safe online.

Junior Achievement
One Education Way

Colorado Springs, CO 80906
(719) 540-8000
Website: https://www
.juniorachievement.org
Facebook and Instagram:
@JuniorAchievementUSA
Twitter: @JA_USA
The organization prepares young people to succeed in business and entrepreneurship efforts by providing programs in financial literacy and economics.

Media Smarts

205 Catherine Street,
Suite 100
Ottawa, ON K2P 1C3
Canada
(800) 896-3342
Website: http://mediasmarts.ca
Facebook and Twitter:
@MediaSmarts
The center supports digital and media literacy and provides programs and resources for homes, schools, and communities in Canada.

National Crime Prevention Council

2614 Chapel Lake Drive, Suite B
Gambrills, MD 21054
(443) 292-4565
Website: https://www.ncpc.org
Facebook: @McGruff
Twitter: @McGruffatNCPC
YouTube: https://www.youtube.com/user/NCPC82

The council helps communities learn strategies to prevent crime, including cyberbullying. They provide training for children and adults in managing situations of cyberbullying.

PACER's National Antibullying Prevention Center

PACER Center, Inc.
8161 Normandale Boulevard
Bloomington, MN 55437
Website: https://www.pacer.org/bullying
(800) 537-2237
Facebook: @PACERs
NationalBullyingPreventionCenter
Twitter and Instagram: @PACER_NBPC

The center provides resources for people experiencing or teaching about bullying and promotes social change, inclusion, kindness, and acceptance.

Project Fashion

Experience America
4556 University Way NE, Suite 200
Seattle, WA 98105
(800) 410-6088
Website: https://fashion.experienceamerica.com
Facebook: @projectfashionla

As part of the Experience America tech summer program, Project Fashion is aimed at giving students experience working in fashion and design.

YEC Young Entrepreneur Council

745 Atlantic Avenue
Boston, MA 02110
(484) 403-0736
Website: https://yec.co
Facebook: @yecorg
Instagram: @YEC

The council is an invitation-only organization for young people interested in starting their own business or becoming entrepreneurs. Find out if you qualify or research the benefits of the organization.

FOR FURTHER READING

Birley, Shane. *How to Be a Blogger and Vlogger in 10 Easy Lessons.* London, UK: Qed Publishing, 2016.

Furgang, Adam. *20 Great Career-Building Activities Using You-Tube.* New York, NY: Rosen Publishing, 2017.

Giacboy97. *YouTube Planning Book for Kids Vol. II: A Notebook For Budding YouTubers.* Milton Keynes, UK: Beans and Joy Publishing Ltd., 2017

Klein, Emily. *From Me to YouTube: The Unofficial Guide to Bethany Mota.* New York, NY: Scholastic, 2015.

Low, Rachel. *Girl's Guide to DIY Fashion: Design & Sew 5 Complete Outfits.* Concord, CA: C&T Publishing, 2015.

Morreale, Marie. *Bethany Mota.* New York, NY: Scholastic, 2016.

Mortenson, Melissa. *Project Teen: Handmade Gifts Your Teen Will Actually Love.* Concord, CA: C&T Publishing, 2014.

Mota, Bethany. *Make Up Your Mind: My Guide to Finding Your Own Style, Life, and Motavation!* New York, NY: Gallery Books, 2017.

Owings, Lisa. *YouTube.* Minneapolis, MN: Checkerboard Library, 2016.

Tashjian, Janet. *My Life as a YouTuber.* New York, NY: Henry Holt and Co., 2018.

Willoughby, Nick. *Making YouTube Videos* New York, NY: John Wiley & Sons, 2015.

BIBLIOGRAPHY

Bliss, Karen. "YouTuber Bethany Mota on Her New Music: 'I Just Want to Blurt It to the World.'" Billboard.com, June 20, 2016. https://www.billboard.com/articles/news/7409054/bethany-mota-new-album.

BUILD series. "Bethany Mota Reveals How Cyberbullying Compelled Her to Start a YouTube Channel." YouTube, June 14, 2017. https://www.youtube.com/watch?v=yJyQ08Sqq-0.

CarlxBen. "How Many YouTube Channels Are There?" sidekick, August 4, 2017. https://sidekickcollab.com/how-many-youtube-channels-are-there.

Cullins, Ashley. "YouTube Star Bethany Mota and Her Father Sued Over Failed Skincare Campaign." Hollywoodreporter.com, August 21, 2017. https://www.hollywoodreporter.com/thr-esq/youtube-star-bethany-mota-her-diva-dadager-sued-failed-skincare-campaign-1031387.

Daily Shuffle, The. "Bethany Mota Announces New Book, 'Make Your Mind Up.'" October 19, 2016. http://www.thedailyshuffle.com/bethany-mota-announces-new-book-make-your-mind-up.

Izon, Juliet. "How Bethany Mota Overcame Cyberbullying." Los Angeles Confidential, May 11, 2015. https://la-confidential-magazine.com/how-cyberbullying-inspired-bethany-mota-to-become-a-youtube-star.

Jung, Helin. "Bethany Mota Says Having 8.8 Million Subscribers Is 'The Same as a Friendship.'" Cosmopolitan.com, June 8, 2015. https://www.cosmopolitan.com/lifestyle/a40061/bethany-mota-internets-most-fascinating.

Kim, Eun Kyung. "Bethany Mota is the YouTube Star You've Never Heard of (But Your Teen Has)." *TODAY*, October 14, 2016. https://www.today.com/style/bethany-mota-youtube

-star-youve-never-heard-your-teen-has-2D11988771.

Mota, Bethany. "Confidence." YouTube, March 24, 2011. https://www.youtube.com/watch?v=8paIwm0nRYc.

Mota, Bethany. "Draw My Life | Bethany Mota." YouTube, May 8, 2013. https://www.youtube.com/watch?v=RywVBJKKlbg.

Mota, Bethany. "First Video :) Mac and Sephora Haul." YouTube, June 12, 2009. https://www.youtube.com/watch?v=h0wCoXVkjGA.

Mota, Bethany. "You're Not Alone." YouTube, April 14, 2010. https://www.youtube.com/watch?v=DC_jLPEF2Gg.

Nagi, Ariel. "Bethany Mota Opens Up About Her New Music: 'It's Easier to Put Feelings Into a Song.'" Seventeen.com, October 27, 2014. https://www.seventeen.com/celebrity/music/reviews/a26956/bethany-mota-music-career-interview.

Ray, Brian. "General Facts, Statistics, and Trends." National Home Education Research Institute, January 13, 2018. https://www.nheri.org/research-facts-on-homeschooling.

Schlossberg, Mallory. "Aéropostale has Been Banking on This YouTube Star to Save It from the Grave." Business Insider, March 16, 2016. https://www.businessinsider.com/bethany-mota-is-aeropostales-only-saving-grace-2016-3.

Seavert, Lindsey. "YouTube Star Bethany Mota Comes to MN to Fight Bullying." USA TODAY, October 20, 2015. https://www.usatoday.com/story/life/2015/10/20/youtube-star-bethany-mota-comes-to-mn-to-fight-against-bullying/74295156.

Seventeen magazine. "Bethany Mota on How She Overcame Bullies and Became the Queen of YouTube." September 10, 2014. https://www.seventeen.com/celebrity/g1183/bethany-mota-pictures.

Smith, Kit. "39 Fascinating and Incredible YouTube Statistics." Brandwatch.com, April 12, 2018. https://www.brandwatch.com/blog/39-youtube-stats.

Think With Google. "YouTube Creator Stories: How Bethany Mota Made Confidence the Must-Have Accessory." May 2014. https://www.thinkwithgoogle.com/marketing-resources /content-marketing/bethany-mota.

TIME staff. "The 20 Most Influential Teens of 2014." Time.com, October 13, 2014. http://time.com/3486048/most -influential-teens-2014.

Van de Wall, Virginia. "Bethany Mota Talks About Being Bullied on 'The Ellen DeGeneres Show.'" J-14.com, April 9, 2015. https://www.j-14.com/posts/bethany-mota-talks-about-being -bullied-on-the-ellen-degeneres-show-55793.

Vlogging Guides. "How to Become a YouTuber in 10 Easy Steps [2018]." January 4, 2018. https://vloggingguides.com/how-to -become-a-youtuber.

White House. "The YouTube Interview with President Obama." YouTube, January 22, 2015. https://www.youtube .com/watch?time_continue=7&v=GbR6iQ62v9k.

YouTube Help. "How to Earn Money from Your Videos." Retrieved October 21, 2018. https://support.google.com/youtube /answer/72857?hl=en.

INDEX

ABOUT THE AUTHOR

Kathy Furgang has been writing educational books for children and teens for more than twenty years. She has written biographies about celebrities, politicians, business entrepreneurs, and historic figures. She also writes teacher guides and science and language arts content for students from preschool to middle school.

PHOTO CREDITS

Cover, p. 1 Mark Davis/Getty Images; p. 5 Jaguar PS/Shutterstock.com; p. 8 sevenMaps7/Shutterstock.com; p. 10 Lorelyn Medina/Shutterstock.com; p. 13 Bob Chamberlin/Los Angeles Times/Getty Images; p. 15 Taylor Hill/FilmMagic/Getty Images; p. 17 David Livingston/Getty Images; pp. 20, 25 FilmMagic/Getty Images; p. 23 Timothy Hiatt/Getty Images; p. 26 Kathy Hutchins/Shutterstock.com; pp. 28–29 Official White House Photo by Pete Souza; p. 33 AbdullahKo/Shutterstock.com; p. 35 paulaphoto/Shutterstock.com; p. 36 Craig Barritt/Getty Images; p. 37 DFree/Shutterstock.com; additional interior pages design elements krystiannawrocki/E+/Getty Images (blue light pattern), Yaorusheng/Moment/Getty Images (yellow background).

Design and Layout: Michael Moy; Editor: Xina M. Uhl; Photo Researcher: Nicole DiMella